HERE'S TO YOU!

HERE'S TO YOU!

354 TOASTS
YOU CAN USE TODAY
FOR PARTIES, HOLIDAYS, AND
PUBLIC AFFAIRS

ROBERT L. GARRISON

Illustrated by Arnie Levin

Crown Publishers, Inc.
New York

To Valda . . .

the toast of my life!

Text Copyright © 1980 by Robert L. Garrison
Illustrations Copyright © 1980 by Arnie Levin

Inquiries should be addressed to
Crown Publishers, Inc.,
One Park Avenue,
New York, New York 10016

Printed in the United States of America

Published simultaneously in Canada by
General Publishing Company Limited

Library of Congress Cataloging in Publication Data

Garrison, Robert L.
Here's to you!: The toast, the universal ceremonial.

1. Toasts. I. Title.
PN6341.G3   808.85'1   80-12049
ISBN: 0-517-540770
10 9 8 7 6 5 4 3 2 1
First Edition

CONTENTS

ACKNOWLEDGMENTS

Early in the collection of material for this book it became evident that people of divers cultures took pride in the customs of their respective countries and were indeed interested in sharing information. This encouragement, along with the cooperation of many knowledgeable groups and individuals, has contributed importantly to *Here's to You!* We would like to express our gratitude for the availability and assistance of these organizations:

The New York Public Libraries
Protocol Office, United Nations, N.Y.
U.S. Department of State, Protocol Office, Washington, D.C.
U.S. Department of State Library, Washington, D.C.
Dag Hammarskjöld Library, United Nations, N.Y.
National Aeronautics and Space Administration, Washington, D.C.
Saint Andrew's Society, N.Y.
The Walter Hampden-Edwin Booth Theatre Collection and Library, The Players, N.Y.
University Club Library, N.Y.
. . . and an especial recognition to the personnel at the UN Mission and Consulate offices of the membership of the United Nations, N.Y.

We also extend our sincerest thanks to these individuals for their inspiration, counsel, and labors:

Eileen McDermott, who provided professional direction and diligence to the research tasks; and to Clare Lynch O'Brien, Carole La Rocca, Randi Goldstein, Barbara Ragan, and Paula Brown; to Charles N. Campbell, Jack Wilcox, Dick Maury, René J. Oulmann, Terry Quinn, and virtually every other friend I have—thanks to all, for their important contributions.

In addition, we would like to express our appreciation to the publishers of collections of toasts, quotations, and related subjects that are listed in a bibliography at the back of this book.

PREFACE

If there's one thing people have in common, and have had since history began, it's the custom of the toast, the practice of drinking to or with someone. Of all the ways of the Earth's inhabitants none is as widely accepted as the tradition of well-wishing.

Toasting has a scattered history. It has touched most civilizations, with notable similarities among the various rituals, save the language in which the toast is made. Research has revealed where and under what circumstances the observance of the toast may have started, and how it developed until today, when toasting is accepted as the habit of welcome and greeting among most of the people and nations of the world.

There are many occasions for toasting—social affairs, religious blessings, the diplomatic scene, and the private moment when one human being exchanges warm, personal wishes with another.

Throughout this compilation, one message will ring out loud and clear: the commonality of humankind—yesterday, today, and, we hope, tomorrow. There's reassurance here that the whole human race can be drawn together by such a simple, unpretentious statement as "Here's to You!"

> Friendship's the wine of life
> Let's drink of it and to it.
> —Anonymous

ORIGINS OF THE TOAST

Once upon a time in a garden called Eden, a man, Adam, and a woman, Eve, met for the first time. There were no words. There were no gestures. But there was a welcome, each to the other. They shared the fruit of the tree in the garden. With this, among other effects, the custom of the mutual greeting took its first form.

From that day, beyond the measure of time, to this, the practice of meeting and partaking of the fruit has been widely accepted among the peoples of many lands.

In the beginning life was not easy. The first inhabitants were looked upon as fair game by the animals who outnumbered them. Their comforts were few. There were no fringe benefits. They dressed in skins and lived in caves. The mere fact of their survival is reason enough for us to admire their ingenuity.

It was undoubtedly during these early troublesome times that the elements of basic companionability were established and the germ of tribal life took shape. From the original nods, grunts, and clouts evolved the sophistication of the amicable sharing of food and drink as we know it today.

Olympian Beginnings

Subsequent roots of the toast are found in Greek mythology. They can be traced to Dionysus, son of Zeus and Semele. Zeus, king of the gods, was regarded by the Greeks as the only god who concerned himself with the entire universe. In this universe were the mortals who inhabited Earth, the land just below Mount Olympus. Among these earthly creatures was Semele, the lovely daughter of King Cadmus of Thebes. Zeus was so taken with her beauty that he changed himself into a man so that he might marry her. The product of their union was Dionysus.

Most tales about Dionysus associate him with uproarious and upredictable behavior, presumably caused by drinking too much wine. His disciples at such festivities included nymphs, satyrs, and attendants called maenads (simply defined as frenzied women!). The life of Dionysus was not all fun and games, however. The Greeks to this day credit him with the development of farming methods used in the growing of grapes and the successful production of wine.

The Romans, successors to the Greeks, also honored the god Dionysus with but one critical alteration. They changed his name to Bacchus, the name more commonly associated with him today. In Roman legend, though, the young god was granted a more dignified role than just god of wine—he was venerated as symbolic of the social and beneficial influences of wine as well.

The Toasting Gambit

It is generally agreed that the tradition of toasting evolved from the formality of the host drinking from the cup first to prove that an offered drink was not harmful. This act generated feelings of trust and good will, leading to the Greek and Roman customs of drinking healths on dining together. The safety factor—that of the host tasting the wine first—was maintained, however. History also relates that both the Egyptians and the Chinese offered wine to guests before eating. In fact, giving the guest a goblet of wine upon his arrival at the host's home was taken as a sign of welcome.

C_2H_5OH

Somewhere along the line, humankind discovered taste sensations, which provided both the thirst-quenching property of water and a relaxing quality that made the liquid seem more palatable. Today this unbender is called alcohol, and it comes in hundreds of flavors, colors, and concentrations.

Before one can undertake a definitive study of the fine art of toasting, one must first dip into the cup, as it were, and explore the values of alcohol as perceived by man and woman:

It usually tastes good.

It is often attractively presented.

In moderation, it has a pleasant yet slackening effect on the senses that gives the imbiber a confidence, a comfort, and a satisfaction not readily available through other means.

And finally, it is and has been an accepted social grace which, even without words, acknowledges a companionability among participants.

It is surmised that in former times, alcohol was primarily used as a preservative for foods and beverages, an important consideration in near-equatorial lands. The discovery of fermentation and its conservative qualities was probably accidental. The detection of alcohol's other virtues was undoubtedly intentional.

There are many people who live in areas of the world where drinking alcoholic beverages is forbidden, or at least is severely frowned upon. These "nonalcoholics" are toasters, too, but not quite to the same degree as their uninhibited counterparts. The libations most often served in such circumstances are coffee, tea, and a variety of soft drinks. But the majority of toasters seem to prefer stouter stuff.

Northern Hospitality

The toasting ritual surfaced with the Vikings, sometime between A.D. 700 and 1000. Though they were the first world travelers, they managed to spend enough time at home to establish an early version of the toast.

In the typical Scandinavian house at that time, especially during the cold winter months, there was always a warming fireplace, enough "frozen" food for the season, a table, benches, and other hand-crafted furniture for comfortable survival. When a traveler was passing through, it was customary for him to be invited into a villager's home to warm up, to rest, and to be refreshed from a bowl of tepid beer that was ever-present on the table. As the tale is told, this bowl was usually offered as a first gesture of welcome. The bowl was called, and is still called, a *skoal*. This word, with minor variations, continues to be the basic Scandinavian expression of the toast.

The word "toast" originated in a different place and at a different time—six centuries later, during one of England's several heydays.

Gentlemen, The Queen!

During the reign of Elizabeth I (A.D. 1558–1603) in Merrie Olde England, few people drank water because it was hardly fit to drink. Beer and ale were the favorite potables and were consumed in vast quantities. Wine was the choice of the more affluent. (It is duly noted that the queen enjoyed both beer and wine with her breakfasts.) There was plenty of wine available, and most of it was stored in wooden barrels, then called tunnes. Since corks were not yet used in bottles, wine had to be consumed quickly or it spoiled. So wine was quaffed rather than sipped. (Perhaps this is the origin of the "bottoms up" feature of toasting.)

To ensure a more pleasant and lasting flavor and to counter the vinegary taste of soured wine, the more imaginative imbibers experimented with spices and other seasonings. The most successful and acceptable method was to add spices to a piece of toasted bread, put the toast in the wine, drink the wine, and then eat the toast. A slice of toast added to a glass of wine, a jug of ale, or a mug of beer furnished the drink with extra nutritional value—and now the factor of health was included. It's reasonable to surmise that the expression "To your health!" arose from such circumstances. "To your health!", one would say on drinking wine with a friend, and then down the drink; "And to yours!", the other would say, finishing off his sopping-wet toast. Customs have started from stranger beginnings, but there is logic to the staging of this one.

The Toast as a Political Device

Here is an example of how the toast has been used by men of letters to promote a point of view, or at least a consideration of same.

It would seem evident that the raising of the glass in a toasting salute would occur with the mention of *the King* in each case.

> *The King!*—can drink the best of wine.
>   So can I;
> And has enough when he would dine—
>   So have I;
> And cannot order rain nor shine—
>   Nor can I.
> Then where's the difference, let me see,
> Betwixt my lord, *the King,* and we?
> If happy I and wretched he,
> Perhaps *the King* would change with me.

—*Differences*
Charles Mackay (1814–1889)

7

The Love Boat

When Cleopatra was regaling Marc Antony on her Nile River barge several centuries ago, the opulence of the feast was overshadowed by the extravagance of her toast. She dropped two perfect pearls into her wine and drank it all down, happy in this tribute which cost more than the entire banquet. Although history does not record her words, it does report that she drank to his health.

Not all the people of England agreed with the concept of toasting as it was practiced then. For example, William Prynne, a Puritan, published a paper in 1628 titled *Healthes and Sicknesses,* in which he attacked the drinking of healths as a pagan rite. The ruling monarch at that time, Charles I, who was no Puritan, concurred with the Prynne statement and issued a royal proclamation that read:

> There are likewise another sort of man
> of whom we have heard much, and are sufficiently
> ashamed, who spend their time in Taverns, Tippling
> Houses, and Debauches, giving no other evidence of
> their affection for us, but in drinking our Health.

It is also recorded that in 1684 Jonathan Robinson, a London bookseller, issued a powerful attack on the custom of drinking healths, which was gaining steadily in popularity. The complete title of his book was:

> *The Great Evil of Health Drinking: or a discourse*
> *wherein the original evil and mischief of drinking of*
> *health are discovered and detected, and the practise*
> *opposed, with several remedies and antidotes against it,*
> *in order to prevent the sad consequences thereof.*

The Tatler, *1709*

By the beginning of the eighteenth century, the custom and the expressions of toasting seem to have become part of the language. In 1709 *The Tatler,* a smart London periodical, published this friendly tale:

> It is said that while a celebrated beauty was indulging in her bath, one of the crowd of admirers who surrounded her took a glass of the water in which the fair one was dabbling and drank health to the company, when a gay fellow offered to jump in, saying, "Though he liked not the liquor, he would have the toast." He was opposed in his resolution, yet this whim gave foundation to the present honour which is done to the lady we mention in our liquor who has ever since been called a toast.

So it has been since time began—the gesture of greeting and of expressing friendship has been with us. What better way to extend this tradition than to utilize one's creative talents in proposing a toast, on any occasion, that is appropriate, thoughtful, and original.

The Toasting Occasions

Today, the ritual of the toast is a common aspect of social functions. At almost every affair, someone is on his feet toasting the bride, the groom, the retiree, the new president, the new child, or the celebration of an accomplishment. And what a pleasant custom toasting is. It compliments the achiever and it provides the toaster with an audience to whom he can lay bare his native talents as writer, speaker, humorist, or dramatist.

Although the toasting procedure is extremely flexible, there are certain guidelines one can follow. Leading authorities on protocol in America are in reasonable agreement as to the appropriate procedures for different occasions.

When asked to function as a toaster at an affair, one must work carefully on the creation or selection of the toast. The toast and its presentation should be looked upon as something special. It should be distinctive. It should be memorable. If the toaster has the ability to compose an original toast, he should do so but it is equally acceptable to use quotations, anecdotes, or stories especially well suited and related to the person or the affair.

Mark Twain credits Adam as the only man who, when he said a good thing, knew that nobody had said it before him. So, in search of suitable quotations to honor the guest, pay heed to Twain's words as well as to the statement of Michel de Montaigne: "I quote others only the better to express myself." Feel free to be generous with an ample display of literary gems in any toast you prepare. Often such a presentation will add distinction to the toast and dignity to the affair, along with a new-found respect for the toaster.

On the next few pages there are examples of toasts along with a few usable quotations arranged by subject and selected to help the toaster in the fulfillment of his task. To personalize the toast is a simple matter. Use an expression such as "So here's to you!" or "I give you the one whom Shakespeare had in mind when he wrote: (quote)," or "And here's living proof of the truth of this quotation—(name of toastee)." In some cases, names and years of authors are included for the toaster who might want to embellish his remarks. Just be sure to add the proper seasoning of sincerity, wit, and creativity, and the toast will surely be a success! Do remember that with any toast, brevity, being the soul of wit, should be gainfully employed.

Staging the Toast

Since a toast has such flexibility in its structure and utility, composers and dramatists have relied to a great degree on toasting as a device in operas and plays. Taking opera as a prime example, toasts are often used to set the stage for the play, to introduce new characters, to develop the story, or just to set up a choral number. Some operas that make use of toasts in one of these ways include *Carmen, La Bohème, The Tales of Hoffman, Hänsel and Gretel, The Bartered Bride, La Traviata, Der Rosenkavalier, Don Giovanni,* and *The Masked Ball.*

Musical comedy has its share of toasting scenes as well, with one of the most memorable of these being the Drinking Song from Sigmund Romberg's *The Student Prince.* In plays and movies there are numerous examples, such as Noel Coward's classic *Cavalcade* which begins and ends with a New Year's toast.

The Unhappiest of Toasts

It depended on the role you played—as participant or observer—to determine whether or not it was a festive affair, but in Caesar's time in ancient Rome, it was best to be sitting in the upper loges. The main act in the arena was the battle of the gladiators, from which only half would walk away. The toast, spoken en masse by all the combatants, with weapons held high, was addressed to Caesar. The words: *"Ave, Caesar! Morituri te salutamus!"* The translation: "Hail, Caesar! We who are about to die salute you!"

PERSONAL MATTERS

In which toasts are shared with friends, and are used in affairs of the heart, family, and other concerns.

Friendship

May we have a few real friends
rather than a thousand acquaintances.

Here's to our absent friends—
God bless them!

To your good health, old friend,
may you live for a thousand years,
and I be there to count them.

—Robert Smith Surtees (1803–1864)

May harmony fill our hearts, not merely
charm our ears.

May we never want for a friend
nor a glass to give him.

Here's to you, as good as you are,
And here's to me, as bad as I am;
As bad as I am, as good as you are,
I'm as good as you are as bad as I am.

                —Old Scottish Toast

May friendship, like wine, improve
as time advances, and may we
always have old wine, old friends,
and young cares.

Here's to those of us who are friends—
and let the rest of the world
make its own arrangements.

Man and Woman

To the ladies, God bless them,
May nothing distress them.

Woman's faults are many
    Men have only two;
Everything they say,
    And everything they do.

You may drink to her eyes, her lips, her hair,
Her form divine, distingué air;
But here's to the girl with a heart and a smile,
Who makes this bubble of life worthwhile.

May all single men get married
And all married men be happy.

Classic Toast by G.B.S.

A renowned host of London enjoyed the company of celebrities whom he would invite as an embellishment to his epicurean dinner parties. The only obligation of the notables was to participate enjoyably in the affair by delivering an original toast when called upon, the subject of the toast having been predetermined by the host.

It is reported that George Bernard Shaw, who rarely passed up a good thing, attended one such party and was called upon to deliver an after-dinner toast on the subject of sex, which at the turn of the century was considered an audacious word. Shaw stood, raised his glass, addressed the guests thus: "It gives me great pleasure . . ." and sat down.

If all your beauties one by one
I toast, then I am thinking
Before the tale were well begun
I would be dead of drinking.

Here's to woman—once our superior,
now our equal!

                                                —1904

Courtship and Love

I drink to one, and only one,
And may that one be she
Who loves but one, and only one,
And may that one be me!

Drink to me only with thine eyes,
    And I will pledge with mine;
Or leave a kiss but in the cup
    And I'll not look for wine.

        —To Celia
          Ben Jonson (1573?–1637)

Here's to our sweethearts and our wives;
May our sweethearts become our wives,
And our wives ever remain our sweethearts.

A Toast of Passion

One of the most unforgettable of love toasts was proposed to Ingrid Bergman (Ilsa) by Humphrey Bogart (Rick) in the 1942 Warner Brothers film *Casablanca*. In its entirety, it reads:
    "Here's looking at you, kid!"

To her whose beauty doth excel
Story, we toss these caps and sell
Sobriety a sacrifice
To the bright luster of her eyes.
Each soul that sips here is divine:
Her beauty defies the wine.

        —Thomas Carew (c. 1595–c. 1639)

I have known many,
    liked a few,
Loved but one—
Here's to you!

Let's drink to love, which is nothing
. . . unless it's divided by two!

Bachelor Party

Here's to our bachelors, created by God
for the consolation of widows
and the hope of maidens.

Here's to life, liberty, and
the pursuit of women!

God made the world and rested.
God made man and rested.
Then God made woman . . .
Since then neither God nor man
has had any rest.

Here's to the man who's rocking his child
And rocking his child alone.
For there are some who rock another man's child
When he thinks he's rocking his own.

Drink ye to her that each loves best,
    And, if you nurse a flame
That's told but to her mutual breast,
    We will not ask her name.

        —Thomas Campbell (1777–1844)

May we never crack a joke
to crack a reputation.

Here's to wives and sweethearts, sweet,
May they never, never meet.

—Army toast, 1918

A full tumbler to every good fellow—
a good tumble to every bad one.

—*In Praise of Ale,* 1888
W. T. Marchant

20

For it's always fair weather
When good fellows get together,
With a stein on the table
And a good song ringing clear.

>   —*A Stein Song* (refrain)
>   Richard Hovey (1864–1900)

Here's to woman
    And her orifice of sin.
It lets her liquefactions out
    And other factions in.

>   —Attributed to Eugene Field (1850–1895)

Here's to the lasses we've loved, my lad,
Here's to the lips we've pressed;
For of kisses and lasses
Like liquor in glasses,
The last is always the best!

To the upcoming marriage: the only sport
in which the trapped animal has to buy
the license.

A very proper Toast
to be used by the Host
when the Intent is
to Close the Bar.

>   "That's all there is;
>   there isn't any more!"

>>   —Ethel Barrymore (1879–1959)
>>   Added, with the author's
>>   permission, as the curtain line of
>>   *Sunday* (1904).

Hail the Bridegroom—hail the Bride!
Now the nuptial knot is tied.

> —*Ruddigore*
> W. S. Gilbert (1836–1911)

To the bride and groom—
> May they have a lifetime of love
> and an eternity of happiness.

May all your pain be sham pain
And all your champagne real.

Happiness to the newlyweds from the oldlyweds.

May your joys be as deep as the ocean
and your sorrows as light as its foam.

To our lovely bride—may your years of
happiness be as plentiful as the teeming
wishes of your bridal showers.

Marriage Toast—Short Form

"Well—here's how . . .
and why . . . and wherefore
. . . and you know where
marriages are made."

> —From *The Animal Kingdom,* by
> Philip Barry (1896–1949)
> copyright, 1931, by Philip Barry

Here's to the bride that is to be,
Happy and smiling and fair.
Here's to those who would like to be
And are wondering when and where.

A toast to the bridesmaids.
>   We adore you for your beauty;
>   respect you for your abilities;
>   honor you for your virtue;
>   and love you . . . because we can't help it!

Ceremonial Toasts

In some marriage observances, a toast is shared by the bride and groom. A nineteenth-century writer, William Heineman, notes that "This pledging each other in wine . . . is nothing more than a survival of the once universal custom of parties drinking together in ratification of a bargain."

With members of the Greek Orthodox Church, for example, the wine cup or glass is broken after the toast. The Greek groom stomps on the glass to break it, saying "May they thus fall under our feet and trodden to pieces, who shall endeavor to sow dissension or discontent between us!"

There is a similar ceremony in the Jewish wedding, but the shattering of the wineglass is in memory of the destruction of the Temple of Solomon.

Here's to our favorite new couple:
>   May all your troubles be little ones.

To the anniversary couple, the perfect illustration of the old adage: A good husband makes a good wife; a good wife makes a good husband.

To you on your anniversary:
May every new day bring more happiness
than yesterday.

To Mother and Dad on their wedding anniversary:
    "We never know the love of our parents
    for us till we have become parents."

        —Henry Ward Beecher (1813–1887)

A toast to the perennial bridal couple:
    "With fifty years between you
        and your well-kept wedding vow,
    The Golden Age, old friends of mine,
        is not a fable now."

            —*The Golden Wedding at Longwood*
            John Greenleaf Whittier (1807–1892)

The Royal Weddings

Toasts at wedding receptions in any level of society are, as a rule, not formal at all, so the toasts are not part of the official record. This was the case at the wedding of Her Serene Highness, Princess Grace of Monaco. According to the private secretary of the princess, the toasts were addressed to the prince and the princess with the same informality as would be observed at the marriage of any two young people.

The former Princess Elizabeth (now Queen Elizabeth II) and the Duke of Edinburgh enjoyed a private reception following their wedding where, once again, there was no record of the toasts or who made them. This information was confirmed by the queen's private secretary.

Brides and grooms, be they royalty or not, share the same privileges with all young people who have exchanged vows. The affair is quite personal, with its audience hand-picked by the participants. There is no need for a record of private expressions, wishes, or toasts—so none is kept.

Home and Family

To your house and home,
where there's a world of strife shut out,
and a world of love shut in.

"Here's to your good health,
and your family's good health,
and may you all live long and prosper."

> —*Rip Van Winkle*
> Washington Irving (1783–1859)

To the new homemaker:
   What is a home but your very own Heaven on Earth?
   Live here long.
   Live here well.
   Live here in happiness.

Here's to life's three blessings:
   wife, friends, and children.

To home and family:
   the father's castle,
   the child's paradise,
   the mother's world.

To the newcomer—
   welcome aboard!
To the parents—
   congratulations!
To the grandparents—
   bask in the sunshine of your happiness.

Do not let your heart grow old
Though birthdays come and go;
To the youthful thoughts keep hold
Then, happiness you will know.

Happy Birthday!

An Annual Affair

The singing toast, recognized in almost all parts of the world, sung to a common tune surprisingly enough, is the one that begins.

"Happy Birthday to You!"

It is such a contagious experience to be in a restaurant when the waiters gather around one happy table, single out one person, present him with a candlelit cake, and break into this song. It's most unusual if the rest of the patrons do not join in. A nice custom. A universal toast.

Dry Toast—or Wet

Drink today, and drown all sorrow;
You shall perhaps not do't tomorrow.

> —John Fletcher (1579–1625)

William Jennings Bryan was once asked
to toast the British Navy. He lifted
his glass of water and said:
"Gentlemen, I believe your victories were
won on water."

> —Reprinted with permission from
> *Reader's Digest,* October 1965

I drink to your health when with you.
I drink to your health when alone.
I drink to your health so often,
I'm now worrying about my own.

It is best to rise from life
as from the banquet,
neither thirsty nor drunken.

> —Aristotle (384–322 B.C.)

May the joys of drinking
never supersede the pleasure of reasoning.

An Old Southern Custom

From Lillian Hellman's great play, *The Little Foxes,* we learn of a most unusual toasting observance:

> "Down here, sir, we have a strange custom. We drink the *last* drink for a toast. That's to prove that the Southerner is always still on his feet for the last drink."

HOLIDAYS

A holiday in any part of the world is a day on which people give recognition to a tradition, an event, a person, a season, or a remembrance. The derivation of the word expresses its holy or sacred beginnings, which are still the key aspect of many holidays, but in the observance of several, the spirit of festivity and celebration seems to have taken over. Wherever you find a change from the daily routine you will also find a reason for the continuing practice of the toast, the universal icebreaker.

Every country has its own special holidays. In this country we officially start out the year with New Year's Day, which is followed by Washington's Birthday, Memorial Day, Independence Day, Labor Day, Columbus Day, Veterans Day, Thanksgiving Day, and Christmas Day. In addition, there are many unofficial holidays that are celebrated in some quarters, such as Saint Valentine's Day, Saint Patrick's Day, April Fools' Day, Halloween, Arbor Day, Bird Day, Flag Day, and Child Health Day.

Other countries have a similar array of holidays but some nations are more celebratory than others. For example, the

Irish observe Saint Patrick's Day. The people of Scotland celebrate Saint Andrew's Day. Canadians honor the queen on Victoria Day. The French remember Bastille Day. In Great Britain, there's Commonwealth Day. Political events are honored in most countries, as evidenced by the celebration of Greece's Independence Day, Italy's Liberation Day, Japan's Constitution Day, Germany's Day of Unity, India's Independence Day, and Russia's October Revolution Day.

Most people welcome the New Year, say good-by to winter, greet the springtime and the harvest, and usher out the old year with a flourish. Humankind just loves a party. And each of these occasions begins with lifted glass in hand, a tribute paid, and a mutual sense of camaraderie. It would almost seem that no matter where you are in the world, any excuse for a tipple is acceptable, but there's more to the toast than that. The toast testifies to man's need for a "time out" every now and then, just to be able to keep up with the next spin of the globe.

New Year's Day

Happy New Year!

Love and joy come to you.
And to you your wassail too,
And God bless you, and send you
A happy New Year.

   —Old English Song

Here's wishing you the kind of troubles
that will last as long as
your New Year's resolutions!

I hereby resolve
To keep my resolutions
And to start them at
    the stroke of twelve.
For who knows better than
    this assembled group
That "procrastination is
    the thief of time!"

Let's drink to our noble purpose,
Then forget it—like always!

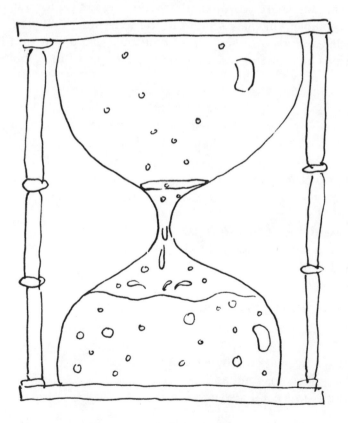

Saint Valentine's Day

To my Valentine:
    "I love you
    Not only for what you are,
    But what I am
    When I am with you."

        —Roy Croft

"Hearts were made to give away
On Valentine's dear day."

        —Annette Wynne

With this toast I pledge you mine.

Here's to love and its day
    of dedication.
May its spirit be with us
    for all our years to come.

Saint Patrick's Day

We'll toast Old Ireland!
Dear Old Ireland!
Ireland, boys, hurrah!

        —Timothy Daniel Sullivan (1827–1914)

May you be in Heaven half an hour
before the devil knows you're dead.

        —Old Irish Toast

I wish you health, I wish you wealth,
    I wish you happiness galore.
I wish you Heaven when you die,
    What could I wish you more?

Here's to health, peace, and prosperity;
May the flower of love ne'er be nipped
by the chill of disappointment; nor
the shadow of grief fall upon us.
But like the green shamrock of
Saint Patrick, may peace and joy
spring from the seeds of contentment.

Let us drink!

—Irish Toast

Mother's Day

To the constant woman who has
    . . . a smile for your joys
    . . . a tear for your sorrows
    . . . a comfort for your failings
    . . . a prayer for your problems
    . . . encouragement for your hopes.
Here's to Mother—on *her* day!

To one whose love does last,
While lesser feelings all have passed,
I lift this toast to no one other
Than she who taught me all—my Mother!

Here's to the prettiest, the wittiest,
The truest of all who are true.
Here's to the neatest, the sweetest,
Here's to them all, Mom—here's to you!

Father's Day

To my Dad, on his day:

"He didn't tell me how to live;
he lived,
and let me watch him do it."

—Clarence Buddington Kelland
(1881–1964)

A wishful toast for all fathers—
"Father of fathers, make me one,
A fit example for a son."

—Douglas Malloch (1877–1938)

To the father of the family on his day
—whose influence is often underrated,
—whose efforts are sometimes overlooked,
but whose persistence and tenacity give
meaning and definition to the whole family.

To Dad—
    from his children who acknowledge
    their good fortune in being blessed with
    a loving and dedicated father.

Independence Day

To one flag, one land, one heart,
one hand, one nation evermore.

    —Oliver Wendell Holmes (1809–1894)

May our counsels be wise,
    and our commerce increase,
May we ever experience
    the blessings of peace.

To America:
    "With all its faults and blemishes, this country
    gives a man elbowroom to do what is nearest
    his heart."

        —*First Things, Last Things*
        Eric Hoffer

Let the tree of liberty thrive
round the world and every one
of God's children share in
its bounty.

Labor Day

May the work that you have
Be the play that you love.

To all who work to live:
    "A truly American sentiment
    recognizes the dignity of labor
    and the fact that honor lies
    in honest toil."

        —Grover Cleveland (1837–1908)

Here's to success, which can set its roots
deep only through soil enriched by
countless failures.

38

George Bernard Shaw wrote the words, and we dedicate
the thought to all who toil on this Labor Day:

> "A day's work is a day's work,
> neither more nor less, and the man who does it
> needs a day's sustenance, a night's repose
> and due leisure, whether he be a painter
> or a ploughman."

To the dignity of labor
and the benefit of its ends.

Veterans Day

To the memory of those
who died for freedom.

To our flag—may its stars light the way
and its stripes guide our steps in the
everlasting cause of peace.

To the land we live in, love,
and would die for.

Thanksgiving

May our pleasures be boundless
while we have time to enjoy them.

Elizabeth, Queen of England (1533–1603)
proclaimed:
> "On Thanksgiving Day no servile labor
> may be performed, and thanks should
> be offered for the increase and abundance
> of His fruits upon the face of the earth."

Let us toast to our blessings and good fortune
on this Thanksgiving Day.

Eat, drink, and be merry,
for tomorrow ye diet.

—William Gilmore Beymer

"To the harvest-time of year
    When Plenty pours her wine of cheer,
And even humble boards may spare
    To poorer poor a kindly share."

        —Anonymous

Happy Thanksgiving to us all!

Christmas

"Christmas is here,
Merry old Christmas,
Gift-bearing, heart-touching, joy-bringing
    Christmas,
Day of grand memories, king of the year."

        —Washington Irving (1783–1859)

Here's to the merriest of Christmases!

"Blessed is the season which engages
the whole world in a conspiracy of love."

        —Hamilton Wright Mabie (1845–1916)

Merry Christmas!

"As fits the holy Christmas birth,
    Be this, good friends, our carol still—
Be peace on earth, be peace on earth,
    To men of gentle will."

            —William Makepeace Thackeray
            (1811–1863)

41

Many happy returns of the day to you—
    No sorrow nor sadness
    But all joy and gladness.
Many happy returns on this Christmas Day!

"God bless us every one!"

        —*A Christmas Carol*
        Charles Dickens (1812–1870)

PUBLIC AND OTHER AFFAIRS

The toast most often used at public affairs over the years—at least the one spoken in greatest numbers—is probably: "Long live the King!" Such a greeting was chanted by the masses at all public appearances of the ruling monarch. With the decrease in the number of royal or ruling families throughout the world over the last century, however, the hue and cry of the masses is now leveled at presidents, directors, prime ministers, sheiks, and other chiefs of state.

At affairs of public significance, toasting is done at the end of the dinner, before the speaker makes his remarks. And then, only the recognized toastmaster offers the testimonial unless he gives permission to other guests.

Depending upon the importance of the circumstance, those extending a toast usually drain their glasses, along with the audience of standing celebrants. The toastee, however, neither touches his or her glass, nor does he stands to accept the honor.

At small dinners, the pouring of the first wine is reason for the host to toast either his guests or the celebration. If the toaster stands, the male members of the company follow suit. There are no formal rules to guide women in these situations, so good judgment prevails. Ordinarily women remain seated, but do participate in the toast.

Dinner at home with friends calls for no formal toasting, but in today's society there is often a recognizable comment, over the first wine, such as:

To your health!

Cheers! To us all!

How pleasant to dine—with friends.

At dinner parties of somewhat larger size, toasts tend to be more traditional and most often are related to the reason for the affair. If one is called upon for a general, rather than a specific toast, the following quotations can be used directly or with minor embellishment:

Let us have wine and women, mirth and laughter,
Sermons and soda-water the day after.

—*Don Juan*
Lord Byron (1788–1824)

I drink to the general joy of the whole table.

—*Macbeth,* III: 4
William Shakespeare

May you live all the days of your life.

—Jonathan Swift (1667–1745)

A health to our friends, our sweethearts, our wives;
May good fortune shine on us all the rest of
our lives.

There are some occasions of this nature in which a response is called for. Unless there are unusual circumstances, such a response is addressed to the host and/or hostess. An example:

> To our host, an excellent man;
> For is not man properly judged
> By the company he keeps?

> To our hostess, a lady of charm
> Which she shares with us in so many ways
> —the appreciative acceptants.

The Toasting Equation

With many people the touching of glasses is a required element of the toast. With others it is not. In this country, at gatherings of limited size, there seems to be a preference for the clinking of glasses, on a one-to-one basis, to convey the personal aspect of the toast. So, with each person clinking glasses once with each of the other participants at a dinner party of twelve, for example, how many clinks to you suppose would have occurred?

As an icebreaker at a party, that's an interesting question to propose, because many people soon forget their algebra on leaving school. But for those who do remember how to solve simple problems, the toasting equation is

$$\frac{n(n-1)}{2},$$

with *n* representing the number of people joining in the toast. At the dinner party of twelve there would be sixty-six clinks. If you don't accept the equation, you can always count out the clinks.

It would take a book in itself to list the many opportunities for toasting. Every day is an occasion. Every cocktail hour can well begin with a toast. Every meeting, every parting, offers the same opportunity.

The testimonial dinner represents a more formal atmosphere for toasting. Someone is honored. People are there to respect this honor. It is a most opportune time for tribute. However great or small the achievement, the toast is rarely overlooked.

To a job well done!

Napoleon, when asked which of his
many armies and troops he considered
best, answered: "Those which are
victorious!"

To the victors!

"Take it for granted that the greater
your achievement the more genuine
will be the surprise of your
friends and neighbors," Joseph
Farrell once said.

On this happy occasion I propose
a toast to you for giving us
this pleasantest of surprises.

Fortunately, you choose not to heed the
statement of W. C. Fields when he said:
"If at first you don't succeed, try, try
again . . . then give up. There's no use
being a damn fool about it."

Here's to you—a veritable tortoise!

The world of business offers abundant opportunities for celebration—hirings, transfers, promotions, and retirements. Particularly with the latter, the numbers increase every day as the mandatory retirement age is lowered and the true and faithful employee is awarded a life of leisure.

Seneca, the Roman dramatist, wrote:
"The gradually declining years are among
the sweetest in a man's life."

May yours be a confection of honeys.

"To be able to fill leisure intelligently
is the last product of civilization,"
said Arnold Toynbee, the great British
historian.

So how can you miss—being one of
the most civilized of all the people
we know. Here's to you!

Occupational Toasts

There are times in the course of one's workaday or social life when one has to assume the role of toastmaster. Such situations happen mostly at informal, unannounced gatherings. If such a nomination falls into your hands, a simple toast can be built around the work, trade, profession, or hobby of the person being recognized. Such a toast should not be wordy or ponderous. Instead, an air of lightness and levity would be most fitting and appreciated. As examples:

To our good friend and neighbor, the finest
practitioner of the do-it-yourself arts who
always manages to hit the nail on the head
—first time!

Here's to the best kind of teacher we know—
who adds class to the classroom, making
normal students want to be exceptional scholars.
What parents could ever ask for anything more?

May I present to you a person who knows
all there is to know about banks—except
breaking and entering.

The world of advertising people is often
referred to as "the jungle." I give
you our very own Tarzan of the Apes.

To our neighborhood doctor whose only
professional problem is to keep
patience with his patients.

Here's to our very own computer technologist
who still uses all his fingers and toes
for the simpler problems of arithmetic.

I give you our legal eagle and counselor
who in the course of his trials has
opened many cases—not all in the courtroom.

Good Luck—Theatrical Style

In the tradition of the theater it is acceptable to wish a player well just before a performance. But since it also the tradition of the theater not to partake of alcoholic beverages before the play begins, toasting with spirits is just not done. Instead, there is an expression, used primarily on opening night: Break a leg! This is looked on as a good-luck wish among professional players.

No one seems to know the origin or history of this phrase, although it is thought to have evolved from the English stage. Lewis A. Rachow, librarian of the Walter Hampden-Edwin Booth Theatre Collection and Library at The Players in New York, suggests: "It is a way to wish an actor well without saying 'good luck.' Theatrical folk are a superstitious lot and they do not like to tempt the gods, so by reversing the wish, the gods will be deceived." And that's how rituals are born.

The Diplomatic Scene

As in any meeting between two people, be they friends, adversaries, or new acquaintances, there is always a preliminary stage in conversation. This initial banter sets the tone of the meeting and clears the air for any discussion to follow. A similar progression is evident in the daily affairs of the diplomat,

who often uses the toast to establish the ground rules for a scheduled meeting.

The toast often announces the positions of the participating parties. It is a significant tool—a door-opener or closer, a friendly handshake, or a rattle of the saber. We should all be beholden to the toast of the diplomat.

The Protocol Office of the U.S. Department of State acknowledges the uses of the diplomatic toast, stating: "It is true that toasts offered at official functions are usually more extensive and significant than the basic requirement for a social gesture would dictate. It is customary that the guest of honor would be toasted by the host in an often lengthy speech and the guest of honor is expected to return the toast with an equally lengthy speech. These usually have considerable political content."

As to the formalities: "It is customary for the host to stand and propose the toast to the guest of honor or to his Chief of State, at which time he asks his guests to join him. The guests stand and raise their glasses for the toast. The guest of honor replies to his host or to the President. Toasts are usually given after the dessert has been served at luncheons, dinners, and banquets. Statements may accompany a toast but this usually depends on the occasion."

The Protocol Office continues: "Whether the guest of honor is the Chief of State or perhaps a Cabinet member of a foreign government, the toast at formal luncheons or dinners is always drunk to the Chief of State (or head of government). The guest of honor should be advised beforehand of the proposed toast in order that he will be prepared to reply. He, likewise, will respond and propose a toast to the President of the United States.

"The person to whom the toast is being given does not partake of the champagne or other beverage at the time the guests lift their glasses in his honor. He usually stands. If the honored guest cannot drink wine, he pretends to do so."

The diplomatic toast reached its apogee on February 21, 1972. On that particular day, the most widely witnessed of all toasts took place. The scene was Peking, China. The host was Premier Chou En-lai of the People's Republic of China. The respondent was President Richard M. Nixon of the United States. The estimated worldwide television audience of viewers of the toast and the response was 400 million people!

The Public Papers of the Presidents, a series of books published by the U.S. Government Printing Office, is a record of the official documents and statements of the Presidents. They include the toasts of the Presidents as well as the responses of visiting dignitaries. Typical of such toasts are these excerpts:

On April 4, 1949, President Harry S. Truman hosted a state dinner in honor of the foreign ministers, ambassadors, and ministers of the twelve countries that had signed the North Atlantic Treaty in Washington. His words:

"May I offer a toast to the Atlantic Treaty
and its success. I think we have really
passed a milestone in history today, and I
think your children and your grandchildren
will tell you that, in the days to come."

Prime Minister Paul Henri Spaak of Belgium responded to this toast, concluding his remarks with:

"I offer a toast to President Truman, and to the American People for their aid and generosity."

●

On April 22, 1960, President Dwight D. Eisenhower hosted a state dinner in honor of President Charles de Gaulle of France. His toast included these words:

"At the end of the war we learned certain things about peace. One is that there is no peace merely because the cannons are still. Another is that many people talk about peace who are not talking honestly except as they conceive of a peace as a condition in which their opponents must surrender their privileges and rights and live in a state of serfdom."

President de Gaulle's response confirmed President Eisenhower's remarks. He then concluded with:

"I raise my glass to President Eisenhower, the Government of the United States, to the American people—the friend and ally of France."

●

On November 21, 1961, President John F. Kennedy toasted Chancellor Konrad Adenauer of the Federal Republic of Germany. His statement was most complimentary to Adenauer and to his efforts with regard to NATO:

> "I think an alliance is an extremely difficult
> system to operate. The interests of all must be
> considered. It is far easier for our adversaries
> to move with speed, commanding as they do their
> satellites. We are all sovereign and allied,
> and we are therefore interdependent as well as
> independent. . . . So I hope that all our guests
> will join me in drinking to one of the transcendent
> figures of our time — the Chancellor."

The Chancellor's response included:

> "I have always considered it to be one of the
> greatest deeds of the American people that after
> having won this victory in 1945, under the
> leadership of the United States of America,
> that the victors did not rebuff the vanquished,
> but on the contrary they extended a helping
> hand—they helped them get back on their feet.
> That, I think, was a great action—a great
> deed—and rare in history. . . . I now propose
> a toast to you, sir, and to the indissoluble
> friendship between the people of the United
> States of America and Germany."

•

On June 25, 1979, during a visit to Japan, President Jimmy Carter proposed this toast on an informal occasion:

> "To peace and friendship among all people."

"General" Diplomacy

The ending of the European hostilities of World War II accounted for a most unusual toast. It took place at the first meeting of the American and Russian generals shortly after the fall of Berlin.

One of the participants, General George S. Patton, Jr., of the Third American Army, was regarded by the Russians as something of a celebrity because of the incredible speed and success of his forces in crossing Europe. Patton did not enjoy the Russians or the occasion. One of the Russians, through his interpreter, invited Patton to join him in a drink. Patton's response,* through the same interpreter was, "Tell that Russian sonuvabitch that from the way they're acting here I regard them as enemies and I'd rather cut my throat than have a drink with one of my enemies."

The interpreter paled. "I'm sorry, sir, but I cannot tell the general *that,*" he stammered in a state of shock. Patton then *ordered* him to translate everything he said, word for word, which the translator did.

The Russian broke into a broad smile, and through the interpreter replied, "The general says he feels exactly like that about you, sir. So why, he asks, couldn't you and he have a drink after all."

This brought a smile to Patton. The Russian continued to grin. They locked arms and drank to each other.

The United Nations

The diplomatic situation at the United Nations is unusual in that it is not as complex as one might suspect. Aside from the ongoing regulation of diplomatic activities, there is a social scene that is somewhat simplified by the UN acceptance of six languages—English, French, Russian, Spanish, Chinese, and sometimes Arabic. All official affairs are confined to the use of

* Quotations from Ladislas Farago's book, *Patton: Ordeal and Triumph* (New York: Astor-Honor, 1964).

any one of these languages, with the Secretary General speaking in English more than in any other language.

As the host of the United Nations, the Secretary General is responsible for the initial welcoming or honoring toast, which is mandatory at most social functions for visiting dignitaries. Ordinarily, he will extend his greeting in the manner of a toast at a reception or a dinner at the proper, socially acceptable time—like before the coffee at dinner, or when the assemblage is complete at the reception. He will propose the toast in English, unless the dignitary speaks another of the six official languages. The Secretary General will speak in English, however, rather than use a language in which he is not proficient.

The libation at all United Nations functions is champagne. However, the preferred drink of the particular person being honored is always determined beforehand. If the honoree is a nondrinker, or from a nondrinking country, mineral water, natural water, or fruit juice is substituted for the champagne. The honored guest speaks for himself and his party only. If other people at the function wish to join in the toast, they may do so by drinking champagne along with the toaster.

The Chief of Protocol of the United Nations summarizes the UN posture in this way: "The rules are quite simple and quite logical. A guest is being honored, so he is honored with proper food, proper drink according to his standards. English is the language most often used because it is the one most universally used at the United Nations and for no other reason."

●

Drink not to my past, which is
    weak and indefensible,
Nor to my present, which is
    not above reproach;
But let us drink to our futures, which,
    thank God, are immaculate.

—Leone P. Forkner

56

TOASTS OF THE WORLD

What better way to perpetuate the gestures of greeting and friendship that toasting expresses than to speak (or try to speak) in the tongue of the beneficiary? Agreed, learning another language is no easy task, but the ability to summon up one or two key phrases at the proper moment is within anyone's grasp. Along with hello, good-by, and thank you, the phrases used as native toasts are among the most important words to know.

When in Roma, for example, it's *Cin-cin!* . . . and in every country of the world there is a pleasant way to ask for friendship.

Most of the toasts listed here translate into best wishes for a person's health or well-being. If a country toasts with an unusual liquor or liqueur, its name is given. The language of the toast is also listed, as well as a phonetic guide to pronunciation. The pronunciations of similar words or phrases may vary depending on the location of the country using the toast. For example, although Algeria is in northwest Africa and Iraq is in the Middle East, both use the Arabic language. However, you will note a different spelling and different pronunciation of the same toast. One logical reason: the two countries are three thousand miles apart, a factor bound to have an effect on any language!

AFGHANISTAN

Be salamati shoma! (Pashto)
(bay-sala-matee shoh-ma)

To your health!

The drink is nonalcoholic, usually a soft beverage.

ALBANIA

Gzuar! (Albanian)
(g-zoo-ar)

All good things to you!

A popular drink is *raki,* or cognac.

ALGERIA

1. *Fi se hetak! (Arabic)*
   (fee say hay-tock)
2. *Se he!* (a common toasting contraction). *(Arabic)*
   (say hay)

1. To your health!
2. Health!

The drink in Algeria, and in most Moslem countries, is coffee, although the Bedouins (nomads) drink tea. Coffee cups are always refilled when empty, but the pourer can be graciously waved off by a slight shaking of the cup. If the cup is held motionless when the pourer offers, it will be refilled.

Toasting is not as common in the Islamic world as it is in the West.

ANGOLA

A sua felicidade! (Portuguese)
(ă soo-ă fay-liss-ee-dădeh)

To your happiness!

The drink is usually wine.

ANTIGUA

Cheers! *(English)*

The drink is rum.

ARGENTINA

Salud! (Spanish)
(sah-lood)

Health!

The drink is *chicha,* among others.
A widely practiced custom in Argentina is
the serving of *maté* to friends
and guests. *Maté* is nonalcoholic, like
tea, and is shared from a common pot with
the participants using indivdual straws, often made of silver. Such an expression as *sirvase un maté* (help
yourself to a *maté)* is part of the tradition.
It is much like a toast among old friends.

ARUBA (Netherlands Antilles)

Salud, amor, dinero, y tiempo pa gozarlo! (Spanish)
(Sah-lood, ă-more, deen-air-o *ee* tee-em-pō pah goh-
zar-lō)

Health, love, plenty of money, and time to enjoy it!

The drinks are all kinds of spirits.
Papiemento is the native language of Aruba. It
is defined as a mixture of Spanish, Portuguese,
Dutch, and a sprinkling of English, French, and Indian.

AUSTRALIA

Cheers! *(English)*
Here's how!
Down the hatch!
Here's looking up your kilt!

The drink is primarily beer, as well as other liquors.

AUSTRIA

Prosit! or *prost! (German)*
　(prō-zit) (prōzt)
May it be to your health!

The drink is beer.

BAHAMAS

Cheers! *(English)*

The drink is rum.

BAHRAIN

Besahtak! (Arabic)
　(beh-sah-tock)

In your health!

The toast is proposed only with alcoholic drink, as
there is no toasting in Bahrain with nonalcoholic
libations.

BANGLADESH

Al salamu alaycum! (Arabic)
　(al salamoo al-aycum)

Peace be with you!

There is no toasting with alcoholic beverages in
Bangladesh, and though the major language is
Bengali, the most often-used greeting is in
Arabic, in the Moslem tradition.

61

BARBADOS

Cheers! *(English)*

The drink is rum.
Although the language is English, it is spoken
with a distinctive Barbadian dialect.

BELGIUM

1. *À vôtre santé! (French)*
   (ă vote-reh sahn-tay)
2. *Gezondheid! (Flemish)*
   (jez-ond-hide)

Both toasts mean: To your health!

The drink is beer. It is rumored that Belgians consume
more beer per capita than any other people.
Another toasting libation is wine.

BENIN

À vôtre santé! (French)
  (ă vote-reh sahn-tay)

All things good to you! is the meaning implied by the
toasters of Benin, although the literal translation is to
your health.

Although the most common language of Benin is
Fon, it is not used in toasting. When the
situation calls for a toast, it is usually made
in French.

BERMUDA

Cheers! *(English)*

The drink is rum.

BHUTAN

Tashi delay! (Bhutanese)
  (tash-*ee* de-lay)

Cheers! or Congratulations!

A popular local drink is *chang,* of which there
are two kinds: *bangcha* (made from millet, wheat,
rice, and corn), and *aara* (a distillation of *bangcha*).
Sincha, a strong liquor made of fermented grain, is sometimes used.

BOLIVIA

Salud! (Spanish)
  (sah-lood)

To your health!

Rum is a popular libation.

BOTSWANA

Witsero! (Tswana)
  (wit-seh-ro)

Long life!

A local drink is *bojwalwa* (a home brew).

BRAZIL

Saude! (Portuguese)
  (să-ood-eh)

To your health!

A popular drink is *cachaca.*

BULGARIA

Nazdrave! (Bulgarian)
   (nahz-drove-eh)

Let us be healthy!

The drink is *slivovitza* (plum brandy).
When toasting in Bulgaria, all glasses are
clicked. If the party is too big, then everyone
touches the table with his glass as a symbolic
clinking.

BURMA

Kyenmabazi! (Burmese)
   (ken-ma-bazz-ee)

Health to you!

A favorite drink is wine.

BURUNDI

1. *À vôtre santé! (French)*
   (ă vote-reh sahn-tay)
2. *Soma! (Rundi)*
   (so-mah)

Both toasts mean: To your health!

The drink can be any alcoholic beverage.

BYELORUSSIAN SOVIET SOCIALIST REPUBLIC

Na zdarowye! (Byelorussian)
   (nahz-drove-yeh)

To your health!

The preferred drink is vodka.

CAMEROON

1. *À vôtre santé! (French)*
   (ă vote-reh sahn-tay)
2. *Mbembe zan! (Ewondo)*
   (mem-bazon)

1. To your health!
2. Enjoy your feasting!

A popular drink is beer.

CANADA

1. Cheerio! Good times! *(English)*
2. *À vôtre santé!* and *À la vôtre! (French)*
   (ă vote-reh sahn-tay) and (ă la vote-reh)
3. *Chimo! (Innuit Eskimo)*
   (chee-mō)

1. Good wishes!
2. To your health! and To yours!
3. Hail!

Popular drinks include Canadian whiskeys and beers.

Eskimo Talk

Although the living isn't easy above the Arctic Circle, the Eskimos of Northern Canada (who prefer to be called Innuits), do have a greeting of welcome and friendship that is well known in the more southerly climes of North America's largest country. The word of greeting is *Chimo!* (pronounced chee-mo). And though it would be unusual for the Innuits to sit around in their icy igloos toasting one another, the sentiment is the same. *Chimo!*

CHAD

1. *À vôtre santé! (French)*
   (ă vote-reh sahn-tay)
2. *Mo doffe! (Sara)*
   (mō-dof-fay)

Both toasts mean: Good health!

A popular drink is beer.

CHILE

Salud! (Spanish)
  (sah-lood)

Health!

Popular drinks are *pisco* (a grape liqueur), and
Chilean wine.

A Chinese Dinner Party

Social drinking in China is looked upon as an expression
of friendship. No cup is ever raised in public without the
acknowledgment of another's in return. Solitary drinking
is just not done. When a person wants to sip his wine
during a meal, he must catch the eye of someone else at
the table, then make the first gesture of the toast. In strict-
est society the cup is raised with both hands before and
after drinking. At less formal parties, the one-handed gesture is acceptable.

A mark of the success of a dinner party is the willing-
ness of the guests to engage in several *kan pei*s, the most
common Chinese toast. A proper *kan pei* is completed
with the overturning of the cup after drinking to show that
the cup is indeed dry.

It is important to keep in mind that the Chinese are not
hurried drinkers. They take their time. They purposely extend the pleasures of the toasting custom, including the
use of small wine cups, which allow for continuing participation.

Chinese Drinking Games

In China, it is customary to serve food with wine, which delays possible intoxication and prolongs the fun and games that are part of most social gatherings. The most common game is *Ts'ai chuan,* which means "guess fist," and is played by two people who attempt to call out loud the total number of fingers each will extend at a given signal. The loser, of course, must *kan pei.* In traditional Chinese fashion, the number is usually called out in a romantic phrase, such as "three bright stars in the sky," or "the four butterflies of the garden." There are often several of these games going on at the table at the same time, which adds to the general merriment.

"Beating the drum to hasten the blooming of blossoms" is another dinner drinking game. A concealed drummer beats a rhythm while the diners pass a filled cup around the table. When the beat stops, the person holding the cup must *kan pei* it. Another cup is then poured and is passed around the table while the beat goes on.

The husband-wife-concubine game causes the greatest laughter. Again it is a game of extended fingers, revealed at a given signal. The "husband" is the thumb, the "wife" is the index finger, the "concubine" is the little finger. As one might suspect in this game, the husband beats the wife, the wife beats the concubine, and the concubine beats the husband. The loser in each situation must commit the wine cup to *kan pei.*

CHINA

1. *Kan pei! (Chinese)*
   (kăn pay)
2. *Yam seng! (Chinese)*
   (yăm sung)

1. Bottoms up! (the most common toast).
2. Drink to victory! (a group-function toast).

The libations vary by region, but *mao t'ai* is the preferred toasting drink.

COLOMBIA

1. *Salud! (Spanish)*
   (sah-lood)
2. *Brindo por . . .* (name of person)! *(Spanish)*
   (breen-doe pore . . .)

1. Health!
2. I drink for . . . (name of person)!

A popular drink is *aguardiente* (distilled sugar cane), or rum.

CONGO

Po na bopeto na uyo! (Lingala)
   (po nah bo-peeto nyo)

For your good health!

A favorite drink in the south is *nsamba* (palm-tree wine), and, in the north, *boganda* (corn wine).

COSTA RICA

Salud! (Spanish)
   (sah-lood)

Health!

Favorite drinks are *guaro* and *chirrite* (both made from sugar cane).

CUBA

Salud! (Spanish)
   (sah-lood)

Health!

The most often-used toasting drink is rum.

CYPRUS

Is iyian! (Greek)
(iss ee-ee-yan)

To your health!

A popular drink is *commanderie* (a liqueur made from Cypriot wines).

CZECHOSLOVAKIA

Na zdravi! (Czechoslovakian)
(nahs drah-vee)

Health to you!

Popular drinks are *slivovice* (plum brandy),
or *borovička* (a liqueur from a native tree).
The social custom in Czechoslovakia is to clink
the glasses while saying the toast.

Good to the Last Drop

At the Prix Danube, a children's television film festival held biannually in Bratislava, Czechoslovakia, the American series "Big Blue Marble" was presented in 1975. Since this was the first U.S. entry in the competition, the producer's party was invited to meet with the festival director and his party. The guests were served *borovička*, a native liqueur, accompanied by many toasts and translated conversation, at the end of which there was a deadly quiet—but no one made a move to leave. In an aside (in English), the assigned translator was asked how to end the meeting properly and gracefully. She said, "You must finish your drink!" And that's the way it is in Czechoslovakia.

DEMOCRATIC YEMEN

Besahetkom! (Arabic)
(beh-sa-het-kom)

In your health! (plural usage).

The libation is usually nonalcoholic.

DENMARK

Skål! (Danish)
(skōl)

A salute to you!

The favorite drink is *akvavit,* also called *schnapps.*

A Danish Nightcap

Many dinner parties in Denmark are topped off by the consumption of "a little black one!" This libation is made by placing a small silver coin on the bottom of an empty coffee cup. Black coffee is then added until the coin disappears from sight. Then, *akvavit* is added to the coffee until the coin, still on the bottom of the cup, again becomes visible. The resultant concoction offers an interesting conclusion to a typical Danish feast.

DOMINICAN REPUBLIC

Salud! (Spanish)
(sah-lood)

Health!

The local drink is generally rum.

ECUADOR

> *Salud! (Spanish)*
> (sah-lood)

Health!

A local drink is *chicha* (fermented corn).

EGYPT

> *Al salamu alaycum! (Arabic)*
> (al salah-moo a-lye-cum)

Peace be with you!

The libation is ordinarily nonalcoholic.

EL SALVADOR

> 1. *A su salud! (Spanish)*
>   (ă soo sah-lood)
> 2. *Salud, vino, y mujeres! (Spanish)*
>   (sah-lood, vee-noh ee moo-hair-ess)

1. To your health!
2. Health, wine, and women! (a male toast).

A popular drink is wine.

EQUATORIAL GUINEA

> *Mba ba sian! (Fang)*
> (ba-ba-see-ahn)

Welcome! (a toast of greeting).

The drink is *malambe* (a liqueur made from palm-tree sap).

ESTONIA

Tervist! (Estonian)
(tere-veest)

Good health to you!

Vodka is a popular drink.

ETHIOPIA

Letanachin! (Amharic)
(let-ana-chin)

To your health!

A common drink is *tella* (made from corn and an herb called *gesho),* or *tej* (made from *gesho* and honey).

FINLAND

1. *Skål! (Finnish)*
    (skōl)
2. *Kippis! (Finnish)*
    (kĭp-pĭss)
3. *Terveydeksi! (Finnish)*
    (ter-veh deck-see)

1. A salute!
2. Cheers!
3. To our health!

Of the three toasts, *kippis* is the most casual and *terveydeksi* is the most formal.
Favorite drinks are: vodka, *sima* (a kind of mead), *akavit* (a strong Scandinavian liqueur), and *mesimarja* (a liqueur from an Arctic berry).

FRANCE

1. *À vôtre santé! (French)*
   (ă vote-reh sahn-tay)
2. *À la vôtre! (French)*
   (ă lă vote-reh)

To your health!

The second toast is the response: And to yours!
The toasting drink of France is champagne.

A French Connection

There are two amusing customs of the French people associated with the conviviality of wining and dining but not regarded as legitimate toasts. One is said when the last drop of wine is poured from the bottle into a person's glass. The expression is *Marié cette année où pendu la prochaine* (Măr-ee-āy set ăn-nay ooh pen-due lah prō-shen). It means "Married this year or hung the next."

The second such custom has to do with the one-gulp consumption of a small glass of a straight liqueur between dinner courses—to clean the stomach, as it were. The phrase used when taking such a drink is *cul sec* (cuy sĕck), which is freely translated as "Bottoms up!" This practice is most common in Normandy, the birthplace of *calvados*.

GABON

1. *Etogo! (Fang)*
   (Ā toe-go)
2. *À vôtre santé! (French)*
   (ă vote-reh sahn-tay)

1. Cheers!
2. To your health!

A popular local drink is *minjok* (a wine of the palm tree).

73

GAMBIA

Cheers! *(English)*

A popular drink is beer.

The Two Germanys

At a proper dinner party in Germany, no one drinks before the host. And it is the host's responsibility to sample the wine before the guests are served. Once all the glasses are filled, the host is still the first to drink. Holding his glass by the stem, he first acknowledges the lady on his right, then all the other guests in turn with *Prosit!* or *Zum wohl!* He drinks; then they drink in response.

Following the initial toast, the guests participate in *Zutrinken,* during which they exchange individual toasts with one another, thus getting the dinner party off to a swinging start. Glasses are only refilled when empty. No verbal response to *Zutrinken* is necessary—the toast has its own etiquette. The person of higher rank initiates the toast and expects a similar compliment in return soon after. The male makes the first move, never the woman, although she is expected to respond in kind. During this exchange, which involves all the guests at the table, there are no words, and no glasses are clicked, but it is apparent that a world of warm feelings and good cheer is shared.

GERMANY—EAST AND WEST

Prosit! (German)
  (prō-zit)
Zum wohl! (German)
  (dzum vole)

To health!—an acceptable meaning for both toasts.

The favorite German beverage is beer. However, wines and *eau de vies* are also used in toasting.

74

The Making of Friends

In many countries of Europe there are two forms of language that can be used—formal and personal—with the choice being determined by whether or not the participants are friends. There are two different verb forms for conversation built around the "you" forms. In French there is the *vous* form (formal), and the *tu* usage (personal). In German there is the *Sie* form and the *du* usage.

There is a toasting ceremony that accompanies the German adoption of the personal form. It is called *Brüderschaft,* which actually means "brotherhood." When two adult males agree to become friends, they drink together in a locked-arm toast, with each usually downing a stein of beer. From this moment on, all their conversation and correspondence uses the *du* form. They have just made *du* and will be friends for life. This experience is not taken lightly.

A German Housewarming

The *Richfest* is the toasting celebration of the building of a new home. When the framework of a new building is erected and set in place, a wreath of pine branches decorated with covered ribbons is hung from the highest rafters. There is an audience for this event, including the laborers, the architect, the future occupants, and their invited guests. The lead carpenter speaks to the assemblage from the top of the framework structure about the pleasure the workers have had in building the house. He also wishes the new owners happiness and asks for the blessings of God. He then drinks a glass of wine for good luck and smashes the glass on the finished structure. The entire group then joins in a celebration, which will be continued either at the new home, if it is adequate, or at a local tavern where there is more drinking, eating, and a series of speeches.

GHANA

1. *Monko! (Fanti)*
   (mawn-kaw)
2. *Na na nom nkwa so! (Twi)*
   (na na nom kwa so)

1. Let it go! (Down the hatch!)
2. A wish for the well-being of ancestors and thanks for having looked after the family!

In Ghana it is customary for people to "pour libation." (See page 102.)
Popular drinks include *nsa fufu* (Akam language) a quiet wine made from palm trees, and *ak pete shie* (a gin).

GIBRALTAR

Cheers! *(English)*
Salud! *(Spanish)*
  (sah-lood)

Good wishes!
Health!

Wine or beer are the most popular
drinks.

GREAT BRITAIN

Cheers! *(English)*

All good things to you!

The most popular toast drink is Scotch whisky, but beer
and wine are sometimes substituted.

The English Pub

England is credited with being the original home of the
pub. The pub is the gathering place where the neighborhood citizenry can meet and talk, or where one can stand
quietly at the bar, to ponder, to recoup one's forces, and
to renew one's substance. Although simply going to a pub
does not necessarily guarantee that a typical, celebratory
toasting situation will take place, there is a communion
that does occur among friends, if present, or with the
publican who pulls the libation. "Cheers!" sets the tone
and the mood of the meeting. After a few pints and a few
rounds of conversation, "Cheerio!" seems a bit livelier. In
either case, the word is almost impersonally spoken when
compared to the more formal and personal toasts of
other countries. However, the Englishman, in an outpour-
ing of sentiment, has been known to look directly at his
compatriot and say with meaning, "To your very good
health!"

GREECE

1. *Stin ygia sou! (Greek)*
   (steen-ee-ya-soo)
2. *Ygia-sou! (Greek)*
   (ee-ya-soo)

1. To your health!
2. Cheers!

The drink is *ouzo* (a licorice-flavored liqueur)
or *retsina* wine.

The Golden Age

Evoe evan! (ay-voy ay-vahn), an ancient Greek toast,
translates freely into wishes for one's health and well-
being. According to the Greek Information Office, it dates
back to before the Age of Pericles (c. 495–429 B.C.) The
expression was also used by Aristophanes in his writings.
It is no longer used among the Greek people, but you
never know what neo-classicists might come up with.

GRENADA

Cheers! *(English)*

At personal affairs—births, weddings, graduations—
toasting is usually done with champagne. On holidays—
the drink is rum.

Other toasts for such celebrations include: Have one on
me! Have a grog! Bottoms up!

GUATEMALA

Salud! (Spanish)
   (sah-lood)

Health!

A favorite drink is *aguardiente* (a sugar-cane liquor).

GUINEA

À vôtre santé! (French)
(ǎ vote-reh sahn-tay)

To your health!

Local drinks are coconut wine, and *sobraqui* (a type of beer).

GUINEA-BISSAU

Cin-cin! (Italian)
(chin-chin)

All good things to you!

The toast is in Italian even though the most common language of this country is a Portuguese Creole.

GUYANA

Cheers! *(English)*

A native drink is a local rum, called *demerara*.

HAITI

À vôtre santé! (French)
(ǎ vote-reh sahn-tay)

To your health!

The most popular drink is rum.

HAWAII

1. *Kamau! (Hawaiian)*
2. *Havoli maoli oe! (Hawaiian)*
   (all vowels, as well as all consonants are pronounced)

1. Here's how!
2. To your happiness!

The drinks are similar to those served in the other American states, except that Hawaiian drinks often include pineapple.

HONDURAS

Salud! (Spanish)
   (sah-lood)

Health!

Rum is the most common drink.

HUNGARY

Egeszsegedre! (Hungarian)
   (eg-geh-segedra)

To your health!

The drink is Hungarian wine.

ICELAND

Skål! (Icelandic)
   (skowl)

A salute to you!

The toasting drink is *schnapps*.

INDIA

Aap ki sehat ke liye! (Hindi)
(ap-key-sayhat-kay-lee)

To your health!

Toasting is not a common practice in India, except
where influenced by the Western world.
Cheers! is an acceptable toast.
The libation in India is usually a soft drink.

India—a United Experience

The tradition and practice of drinking and toasting are not
quite native to India. As a matter of fact, the English words
"To your health!" and other similar expressions are used
verbatim in some parts of India today and are also translated into various Indian languages and dialects. It may be
mentioned that the practice of toasting is more or less
confined to the sections of Indian society that have come
into closer contact with Western culture and traditions.

INDONESIA

Sĕlamat! (Indonesian)
(say-lamat)

To your health!

The beverages are usually soft drinks.

IRAN

Be salamati! (Persian)
(bay salam-atee)

To your health!

One popular drink is *arak* (a raisin-based liqueur). However, most libations are nonalcoholic.

IRAQ

1. *Asslam alaiykum! (Arabic)*
   (as-slam a lye-eh-kum)
2. *Bisahatik! (Arabic)*
   (bess-ah-hatik)

1. Peace be with you!
2. To your health!

A special drink is *arak*, but the most common drinks are soft, and include coffee and tea.

IRELAND

Slainthe is saol agat! (Gaelic)
(slawne-cheh-iss sole-agat)

Health and life to you!

The drink is Irish whiskey.

A Touch of Ireland

The Irish are an artistic people, particularly skilled as writers and tellers of stories. Few national groups are as articulate and imaginative in the use of language. When speaking English, the Irish have a lilt to their accent, known as a brogue. About one quarter of the Irish have a second language, Gaelic, which is a form of the original Celtic language. Gaelic is the tongue of the traditional toast of Ireland:

> *Slainthe is ao agat*
> *Bean ar do mhian agat*
> *Paiste gach bhliain agat*
> *Talamh gan cios agat*
> *gob fliuch*
> *agus bas in Eirinn!*

And its translation:

> Health and life to you,
> Land without rent to you,
> A woman of your choice to you,
> A child every year to you,
> A wet beak [i.e., may you not lack for a drink],
> And may you die in Ireland!

The Irish alone are given credit for poteen, or potheen, a bootleg whiskey which defies description other than to liken it to moonshine. Of poteen it has been written, "You may drink your poteen hot from the still, or, if you are a man of continence you may wait till it cools."

Another of Ireland's notable discoveries, which the world has taken to its bosom, is Irish coffee. There's nothing quite like it anywhere. It's a fine nightcap. It must have been brewed by the leprechauns.

ISRAEL

L'chaim! (Hebrew)
(le kh-ay-em)

For life!

A popular drink is wine.

It's a Small World

The origin of the most often-used Italian toast—*Cin-cin!*—has been traced back to China. According to the *Istituto Italiano di Cultura*, it came from Peking, where *ching-ching* is accepted as a polite expression of gratitude. This statement then passed from the pidgin English of the Chinese traders into an English slang that was later introduced into Italy by Italian naval officers. It is a friendly, casual remark, with no literal translation, usually shared over an informal drink.

ITALY

1. *Alla tua salute! (Italian)*
   (al-la too-uh săl-oo-tay)
2. *Cin-cin! (Italian)*
   (chin-chin)
3. *Prosit! (Latin)*
   (prō-zit)
4. *Propino tibi! (Latin)*
   (prō-pee-no tǐ-bee)

1. To your health!
2. All things good for you!
3. A Latin word used to greet a Catholic priest on his return from the Mass.
4. I drink to you!

Favorite drinks include a wide variety of wines—red, white, and sparkling.

IVORY COAST

1. *Ecielike! (Baule)*
   (ay-see lye-kee)
2. *Yako! (Baule)*
   (yah-ko)

1. Welcome!
2. Be in good health!

The native drink is *m'me* (a palm-tree extract).

JAMAICA

Cheers! *(English)*

All good things to you!

The usual drink is rum.

JAPAN

Kan pai! (Japanese)
   (kan-pīe)

Bottoms up!

The drink is *sake* (a rice wine).

The Japanese people, once rigidly ruled by feudal shoguns, had little opportunity for celebration save their own family gatherings. As a result, toasting healths, collectively or individually, became a source of social entertainment.

"I do," Japanese style

In Japan marriage is an eternal commitment. Almost 94 percent of all adults are married, and there is little divorce. To this day, many marriages in Japan are arranged by the fathers. The Shinto ceremony itself is a profoundly personal family affair that is rarely shared with outsiders. It usually lasts about twenty minutes, and includes chants, prayers, and dances of ritual purification performed by the priests and priestesses. First the bridegroom and then the bride, in turn, take sips of *sake* three times during the service, building up to the final vows, which the bridegroom recites. The bride simply speaks her given name as testimony of accord. The confirmation of the wedding is a toast of *sake,* with the newlyweds drinking from the same *sakazuki* (cup) before joining in with all the relatives and friends in attendance. Chances are that the bridegroom will kiss the bride for the first time that night.

JORDAN

Besehtak! (Arabic)
(bess-ay-tack)

To your health! Good luck! Success! Happiness!

The drink can be alcoholic or nonalcoholic.

KENYA

1. *Kwa afya yako! (Swahili)*
(kwa afee-ya yah-ko)
2. Cheers! *(English)*

    To your health!

A favorite drink is *pombe* (a beer made of honey, flour, and water).

KOREA—NORTH AND SOUTH

1. *Yeuki dang sin! (Korean)*
(yew-kee tung-shin)
2. *Gun bai! (Korean)*
(kun buy)

1. Here's to you!
2. Bottoms up!

A popular drinks is *sauju* (a rice wine).

Korea—North and South

There are three varieties of spirits in the Koreas—*t'akju,* a light wine; *yakju,* a stronger variety; and *soju,* a strong spirit that burns the stomach. One form or another of these liquors is served at funerals, marriages, at sixty-first birthdays,* and ceremonial festivals. On such occasions only married men and women over fifty-five years of age are supposed to participate, but the rules are loose. Young men do drink at these functions, but they turn their backs to their elders so as not to offend them. Young women are permitted a sip. Koreans have a reputation for enjoying wines and spirits, but not to excess—according to their definition: A man is not considered intoxicated if he can still move an arm. *Gun bai!*

KUWAIT

Be seh hettac! (Arabic)
(bay say het-tak)

To your health!

Ordinarily, the drink is nonalcoholic.

LAOS

Xuen dum! (Lao)
(zen doom)

Let's drink!

A local drink is *soum soum* (a rice wine).

---

* In Korea, you are one year old at birth, so at sixty-one your sixtieth year on Earth is being celebrated. In addition, the zodiac allots five years to each of its twelve signs and at sixty-one (sixty years on Earth) you will have completed one full cycle of the zodiac calendar. Seems like a logical time for a toast.

LEBANON

Sihitak! (to a male) *(Arabic)*
  (say-hee-tack)
Sihitik! (to a female) *(Arabic)*
  (say-hee-tick)
Sihatikom! (to a group) *(Arabic)*
  (say-hat-ee-kom)

To your health!

One drink is *arak,* but soft drinks are used at most native occasions.

LESOTHO

Ke u lakaletsa katleho! (Sotho))
  (kay ō laka-let-sah kăth-lay-hō)

Good wishes!

The drinks are beers, wines, and liquors.

LIBERIA

Cheers! *(English)*

The drinks are customarily the same as those used in Western countries.

LIBYAN ARAB REPUBLIC

Al sahetic! (Arabic)
  (al sah-hey-tick)

To your health!

Most drinks are nonalcoholic, but wines are sometimes used.

88

LIECHTENSTEIN

Prosit! (German)
(prō-zit)
Auf ihre gesundheit! (German)
(Ow-ff eer-eh geh-zund-hite)

Both toasts are: To your health and well-being!

The major libation of the country is beer.

LITHUANIA

I sveikata! (Lithuanian)
(ee-svey-ee-kata)

To your health!

The drinks are *midus* (mead), wine, and *aqua vitae* (a liqueur).

LUXEMBOURG

Gesondhét! (Luxembourgeois)
(geh-zund-teed)
Prost! (Luxembourgeois)
(pro-zt)

May it be good for you!

The drinks are beer, Moselle wines, and various liqueurs. Glasses are clicked for toasts in Luxembourg.

MACAO

Tso' nei kinho! (Cantonese)
(tsō nay keen-ho)

To your health!

Rice wines are quite popular.

MADAGASCAR

À vôtre santé! (French)
(ă vote-reh sahn-tay)

To your health!

Two popular drinks are *ranonampango* (a roasted rice wine) and *betsabetsa* (a fermentation of distilled honey).

MALAWI

Kalibu! (Nyanja)
(kal-*ee*-boo)

Come and join me!

Native drinks include *mowa wa masese* (made of corn and cassava root) and *kachasu* (made of sugar and corn husks).

MALAYSIA

Yam seng! (Malay)
(yăm sung)

To good times! (note that China uses this same expression as a victory toast).

A favorite drink is *toddy* (made from the coconut palm).

MALDIVES

À vôtre santé! (French)
(ă vote-reh sahn-tay)

To your health!

The most common language of the Maldives is *Divehi,* but for toasting, French is used.

MALTA

Evviva! (Maltese)
(*ee*-viva)

To your health!

Normally the drink is wine.

MARTINIQUE

À vôtre santé! (French)
(ă vote-reh sahn-tay)

To your health!

The most popular drink in this part of the world, where much of it is made, is rum.

MAURITANIA

À vôtre santé! (French)
(ă vote-reh sahn-tay)

To your health!

MAURITIUS

À vôtre santé! (French)
(ă vote-reh sahn-tay)

To your health!

MEXICO

Salud! (Spanish)
(sah-lood)

Health!

An exclusively Mexican drink is *pulque* (made from fermented cactus plant); another is *tequila* (made from the juice of the maguey plant).

91

A Mexican Contribution

Hats must be doffed to Mexico in particular for its spirited contribution to the world of toasting. It's not the Mexican toast that's unique; it's the toasting beverage. *Tequila* is a strong, fiery liquor made from the juice of the maguey plant grown in the state of Jalisco, near the city of Guadalajara. Even the aficionados, who drink their *tequila* straight, follow this ritual: First, an ample pinch of salt is licked from the crease made in the back of the hand by the thumb and forefinger; then *tequila* is taken neat, from a one- or two-ounce glass held in the other hand; and then a wedge of lime, held in the fingers of the first hand, is bitten into as quickly as possible. This is not a recommended toasting procedure, since talk is difficult for most after a swig of straight *tequila*.

MONACO

À vôtre santé! (French)
(ă vote-reh sahn-tay)

To your health!

The Monegasques, like the French, prefer champagne for toasting, but will make do with almost any libation.

MONGOLIA

Tany eruul mendiin tuloo! (Mongolian)
(tanny erool mendin tulaw)

To your health!

The preferred drink is *arkhi* (a Mongolian vodka).

MOROCCO

Sahtek! (Arabic)
(sah-tek)

To your health!

Soft drinks are the usual fare.

NEPAL

Swasthya! (Nepali)
(swaz-thee-ya)

Good health! Prosperity! Happiness!

Beer, wine, and liquors are acceptable drinks for toasting.

NETHERLANDS

1. *Op je gezondheid! (Dutch)*
   (ōpe yeh khe-zund-hīte)
2. *Proost! (Dutch)*
   (prō-st)

Both toasts mean:
To your health!

A popular local drink is *jenever* (Dutch gin).

NEW ZEALAND

Cheers! *(English)*

All good things to you!

The New Zealanders' favorite libation is beer,
but wines, liquors, and liqueurs are tolerable.

NICARAGUA

Salud! (Spanish)
  (sah-lood)

Health!

An often-used drink in toasting is *flor de cana*
(a local rum).

NIGER

Cheers! *(English)*

A native drink is *burukuto,* brewed from Guinea corn.

NIGERIA

1. *Kedu! (Ibo)*
   (kay-doo)
2. *Kedu maka ndi ulo! (Ibo)*
   (kay-doo ma-ka-dee-oolo)

1. How are you?
2. Regards to your family!

Toasting is not a custom in Nigeria, but the above phrases
are expressions of friendship.

All spirits are enjoyed when toasting.

NORWAY

Skål! (Norwegian)
   (skōl)

A salute to you!

Aquavit is a favorite Norwegian drink for toasting.

PAKISTAN

Khush emded! (Punjabi)
(kush-ahm-ded)

To you!

A popular local drink is *lassi* (a beverage of
yogurt, water, and sugar).
"Cheers!," the English-language toast, is quite
common in Pakistan.

PANAMA

Salud! (Spanish)
(sah-lood)

Health!

Wine and other liquors are used in Panama.

PAPUA NEW GUINEA

Cheers! *(English)*

The drink is usually wine, sometimes champagne.

PARAGUAY

Salud! (Spanish)
(sah-lood)

Health!

A drink that is often used is *canna* (a native brandy).
Salud! is used in both languages of Paraguay,
Spanish and Guarani.

PERU

Salud! (Spanish)
(sah-lood)

Health!

A toasting drink is *disco* (a grape-based brandy).

PHILIPPINES

Mabuhay! (Pilipino)
(mah-boo-hay)

Long life!

To celebrate a toast, the drinks may be champagne, or wine, or *tuba* (a fermented palm juice).

POLAND

Na zdrowie! (Polish)
(nahz-drov-ee-eh)

To your health!

Polish vodka is the odds-on favorite.

PORTUGAL

1. *A sua saude! (Portuguese)*
   (ă soo-ă să-ood-eh)
2. *A sua felicidade! (Portuguese)*
   (ă soo-ă fay-liis-ee-dădeh)

1. To your health!
2. To your happiness!

Without question, the favorite libation is port wine.

QATAR

1. *Be is-Mallallah! (Arabic)*
   (bay iss mal-al-ah)
2. *A-salam alykum! (Arabic)*
   (a-salam a-lye-cum)

1. In the name of God! (used as a toast).
2. Peace be unto you! (a greeting).

The drinks are nonalcoholic—soft drinks or water.

Harvest in Portugal

The harvesting of grapes for the making of port wine involves a three-week celebration near Oporto that is carried on in a spirit that would delight the heart of Bacchus. Men and women of the neighboring villages of the valley are invited to the vineyard, where the grapes are collected and trampled, and the wine-making process begun. All this activity is carried on with the festive accompaniment of music, singing, dancing, and many, many toasts or *vivas* to the grapes, to the vineyard, to Portugal, to England (prime customer for port wine), and to the celebrants, who end up toasting each other.

N.B. We have Portugal to thank for the cork, without which wine would be a most perishable commodity.

ROMANIA*

Noroc! (Romanian)
(nor-rock)

Good luck!

A popular local drink is *tuica* (a plum brandy).

RWANDA

1. *Ku buzima bwacu! (Rwanda)*
(koo-buz-ee-ma wack-oo)
2. *Ku busima bwanyu! (Rwanda)*
(koo buz-ee-ma wan-yoo)

1. To your health!
2. At your health!

A favorite portion for toasting is *urwagwa* (a banana liqueur).

---

* Although Romania and Rumania are both acceptable, the former is preferred by the UN, the U.S. Bureau of Geographic Names, and by the Romanians.

SAN MARINO

Salute! (Italian)
(sal-oot-tay)

To health!

The preferred native drink is a sparkling muscatel, *Moscato di San Marino.*

SAUDI ARABIA

1. *Hanian! (Arabic)*
   (han-ee-yan)
2. *Bialsiha wa alhana! (Arabic)*
   (byal-see-ha wa al-hana)

1. Congratulations!
2. With health and contentment!

The drinks are nonalcoholic—coffee, tea, and soft drinks.

SCOTLAND

1. *Slainte (Scottish Gaelic)*
   (slan-chĭ)
2. *Slainte Mhoiz (Scottish Gaelic)*
   (slan-chĭ vore)
3. *Sailthe eh-vit doch slainte eh lunt! (Scottish)*
   (sayle-thee ay-vit dock slan-chĭ ay lunt)

1. Health!
2. Good health!
3. Hail to you! I leave you with a toast to your good health!

Scotch whisky is the drink. No substitutions, please.

What's in a name?

There's Scotch whisky and Irish whiskey, which differ not only in taste but also in the spelling of the generic name. The difference is intentional and defensible to both Scots and Irish, though neither seems able to account for the discrepancy.

The Scottish Toasts

Slainte! (slan-chĭ) means "Health!" but a more generous toast often said on parting is: *Sailthe eh-vit doch slainthe eh lunt!* (sayle-thee ay-vit dock slan chĭ ay lunt), which means "Hail to you! I leave you with a toast to your good health!" There are additional toasting traditions attributed to the Scottish people that are worthy of note: the loving cup and the stirrup cup.

The loving cup, a symbol of assorted meanings, is also called the grace cup. In former days there was a practice that consisted in offering a cup of choice wine at the very end of a dinner, after grace. The gesture was indeed a bribe to keep the lusty Scots in line during the grace following a laird's banquet or feast. The practice was successful, because the wine served in the cup was always the best of the evening.

Once grace was said, the master of the banquet would drink to his guests. A sizable covered cup, usually made of pewter or silver, would then be passed around the table. Each guest in turn would rise and bow to the neighbor on his right, who would then rise, remove the cover with his right hand, and hold it while the other would drink, using both hands.

The proper use of rights and lefts is critical in this procedure. The reason for the ceremonial goes back to the days of Edward the Martyr, A.D. 963–978. While he was quenching his thirst at the door of Corfe Castle, one of his mother-in-law's servants, whose right hand was not in full view, treacherously stabbed Edward in the back. To prevent the recurrence of such disloyalty, a cover was provided for all manner of drinking cups, and "rules of the game" were established.

The stirrup cup of several centuries ago has its counterpart in the "one for the road" of today. Its origin can be traced back to the *poculum boni genii,* the "drinking cup of good spirits" of the Romans, which was the last cup quaffed at the eating board prior to a general departure. The problems of contemporary living and driving have almost banished this practice from most lands, but it is still observed by the Scots and the Irish, who continue to offer the cordial stirrup cup to their departing neighbors—who probably walk home.

This custom is meticulously adhered to today when a cup of wine or other liquor is handed to the mounted leader of a hunt at the beginning of a day's chase. This tradition is quickly followed by the first cry of "Yoicks!," which urges the hounds on in pursuit of the fox.

SENEGAL

1. *Yalla na ress gam! (Wolof)*
   (yal-ana ress gam)
2. *À vôtre santé! (French)*
   (ă vote-reh sahn-tay)

1. Drink this in peace!
2. To your health!

The drinks in the major cities are spirits, and the toast is *à vôtre santé!* In other parts of the country the drink is water.

A West African Custom

There is a tradition in many of the countries of West Africa called "to pour libation." This practice is usually reserved for ceremonial occasions, such as a meeting with the chief, a visit to a family grave, or a funeral. The gesture itself involves the pouring of some or all of the beverage about to be consumed on the ground. This is an acknowledgment of the presence and remembrance of ancestral spirits, an important aspect of the lives of these people. The amount of liquid poured is determined by the magnitude of the occasion. The drink is often strong—gin or *schnapps.*

SIERRA LEONE

Cheers! *(English)*

Be of good spirits!

A favorite drink is called diamond gin (a distilled palm wine).

SINGAPORE

Yam seng! (Chinese)
(yăm sung)

To your continuing success!

A popular drink for celebrations is brandy.

SOUTH AFRICA

1. Cheers! *(English)*
2. *Gesondheid! (Afrikaans)*
   (khuh-sond-hite)

To your health!

The drinks are beers, wines, and liquors.

SPAIN

Salud! (Spanish)
(sah-lood)

To your health!

Most popular drinks are Spanish wines or brandies.

The Foot Bath

An old Spanish custom not often observed today involves the pouring of wine. This convention was reported by William Heineman in *Manners, Customs and Observances,* published in London in 1894.

Stinginess forms no part of the Spanish character. Without what is called "The Foot Bath" no Spaniard would think of serving or of accepting a drink. When a person calls for a glass of wine or liqueur it is customary for the waiter to fill it up until it overflows into the saucer. This is done to show an excess of liberality.

103

SRI LANKA

Ayubowan! (Sinhalese)
  (eye-you-bow-an)

The toast is a welcome or greeting.

The drink is most often tea, but could be *arak*
(a distilled *toddy*).

SUDAN

Salamo alaykom! (Arabic)
  (sal-amo al-eye-com)

Peace be upon you!

The drink is usually nonalcoholic.

SURINAM

Prost! (Dutch)
  (prō-st)

May it be to your health!

Favorite drinks are rum and gin.

SWEDEN

Skäl! (Swedish)
  (skōl)

A salute to you!

The most popular libation is *akvavit,* with or
without a beer chaser.

Skäl! in Sweden

In what is perhaps the most personal of all toasting rituals, the Swedish *Skäl!* brings people into a moment of close, one-to-one participation. The toaster, sitting or standing, raises a full glass in his right hand to the point at the chest where the third button down on a military tunic would be located. The toaster's eyes seek out a companionate partner, using the raised glass and brooding gaze as a veritable beacon. On making visual contact, both parties share the slightest of smiles, a nod of the head, and *Skäl!* is said. With a twinkle in response, the libation is drained if it is *akvavit*, sipped if it is wine. The glass is lowered to the starting position, the eyes lock again, followed by another friendly nod, and the ritual is completed.

In the course of a typical dinner party the host first *Skäls* all the guests in one fell swoop. With this opening gun fired, the guests are expected to return the courtesy to the host as well as to *Skäl* each of the other guests. There's a special set of rules governing the hostess, who is not expected to engage in the ceremony. She is required to make token responses not to one individual but to several at a time, thus cutting down on her alcoholic intake and lessening the risk of burned biscuits.

SWITZERLAND

1. *Prosit!* or *Gesund wohl! (German)*
   (prō-zit) or (geh-zund-vōle)
2. *À vôtre santé! (French)*
   (ă vote-reh sahn-tay)
3. *Salute! (Italian)*
   (săl-oo-tay)
4. *Viva! (Romansch)*
   (vee-vah)

The toasts all mean: To your health!

The drink of Switzerland is often an *eau de vie,* like kirsch.

SYRIAN ARAB REPUBLIC

Bisatek! (Arabic)
(biss-ă-teck)

To your health!

The drink is sometimes *arak* (a brandy), but most often it is a soft drink.

THAILAND

Chai yo! (Thai)
(ch-aye yoh)

To your health and well-being!

The drink is *mekont* (a whisky, similar to Scotch).

Greetings from Thailand

When Thais meet one another, they do not shake hands. The traditional greeting is the *wai*, with hands raised together as in prayer. It is customary that the higher the hands are held, the more respectful the *wai*, so that the respective ranks of the greeters can readily be noted.

TOGO

Laminesee! (Eze)
(la-minny-say)

To your health!

TRINIDAD AND TOBAGO

Cheers! *(English)*

All things good to you!

A favorite libation is rum.

TUNISIA

Fisehitak! (Arabic)
(fis-ay-itek)

To your health!

The drink is sometimes Tunisian wine, but more often a nonalcoholic beverage.

TURKEY

Serefinize! (Turkish)
(ser-ay-fin-eeze)

To your honor!

A favorite potion is *raki* (a grape-based liqueur).

UGANDA

Kwa afya yako! (Swahili)
(wah afyay yăko)

To your health!

An accepted libation is *maragi* (a combination
of banana, sugar, and fermented grain).
Swahili is spoken in most East Central African countries.

UKRAINIAN SOVIET SOCIALIST REPUBLIC

Na zdorovya! (Ukrainian)
(naz drove-ya)

Good health!

Most often the drink is wine, vodka, or Ukrainian
champagne, depending on the occasion.

U.S.S.R. (Russia)

Za vashe z-dorovye! (Russian)
(ză-vash-drove-yeh)

To your health!

The most widely used drink is vodka.

UNITED ARAB EMIRATES

Yashrab nakhb! (Arabic)
(Ya-shrub nakh)

Drink a toast!

The libation is nonalcoholic.

UNITED REPUBLIC OF TANZANIA

Kwa afya yako! (Swahili)
(wah afyay yăko)

To your health!

The drink is usually beer or spirits.

UNITED STATES OF AMERICA

Here's to you! *(English)*

The native drink is bourbon, but all spirits
are used in toasting.

UPPER VOLTA

À vôtre santé! (French)
(ă vote-reh sahn-tay)

To your health!

Although the native language is *More*, the toasting
wishes are in French.

URUGUAY

Salud! (Spanish)
(sah-lood)

Health!

The most popular drinks are *grappa, cana, ron,* cognac.

VENEZUELA

A la Salud! (Spanish)
(ă la sah-lood)

To health!

A major drink is rum.

VIETNAM

Van tho! (Vietnamese)
(van-dhō)

Long life!

WALES

Iechyd da i chivi! (Welsh)
(yock-eed tha ee skivee)

To your health in drinking!

Beer is the favorite drink of Wales.

YEMEN

Bi sihatek! (Arabic)
(bee say-ha-teck)

For your health!

The drinks are nonalcoholic.

YUGOSLAVIA

Ziveli! (Serbo-Croatian)
(zhiv-elli)

To your health!

A popular drink is *slivovica* (a blue-plum brandy).

ZAIRE

Be twa bu! (Tshiluba)
(bay twa boo)

Welcome to everybody!

The drink is *maluvo akapia* (a distilled corn liquor).

ZAMBIA

Leza abe andinywe! (Tonga)
(lee-za abe-bay andee-nye-weh)

God bless you!

Favorite drinks are the excellent Zambian beers *shibubuko, mosi,* and *muchinga.*

A TOAST FOR TOMORROW

To predict the future, one must first look to the past. There one will find the customs that have been accepted as well as those that were not. Such a review will probably confirm that the tradition of the toast, which has been in vogue since early times, will continue well into the future. There will be changes, of course, as there are with all things, but the basic exchange of wishes—for health, for wealth, for happiness—should survive as long as human beings agree to share this beautiful planet.

One alteration in the toasting ritual is evidenced by the changing status of women over the past fifty years. Toasts from the literature of the last few centuries abound in exalted references to women, to their beauty, and to their desirability. There is a tendency in more contemporary comment to shy away from such overtures. No longer do women want to be placed on pedestals by aspiring males. They would prefer to be honored for their accomplishments and achievements instead.

Another forecast about tomorrow's world is that its main

events will be played on a bigger stage. It is relatively safe to say, at least according to the scientific community, that space is here to stay and that humankind's arena of activity will be expanded. Man and woman will be there—residing in space colonies—to celebrate the events. It is expected that the first such colony may be space-borne early in the twenty-first century, and that by the time that century is over they will be plentiful.

July 17—Rendezvous

One of the more unusual greetings ever exchanged took place at the meeting of the teams of the U.S.A. *Apollo* and U.S.S.R. *Soyuz* in space in 1975. In this joint venture, Russians and Americans agreed to dock (join) the two capsules in space so that the crews could meet, talk, and eat together. When the joining was complete, the Americans crossed over into the Russian module and shook hands. The rendezvous took place at 225 kilometers above the city of Metz, France.

Although there were no formal toasts or grand speeches, there were handshakes all around. In the background of the Russian craft was a hand-lettered sign in English: "Welcome aboard Soyuz."

Congratulations to the space crews were offered by Leonid Brezhnev and President Gerald R. Ford via the air-to-ground link.

Many predictors do not foresee great changes in the customs of mankind during this same period, so it is assumed people will continue to observe Earth-time and will celebrate birthdays, weddings, holidays, and the same kinds of affairs that were shared yesterday and are still shared today. Toasting will undoubtedly survive. The expressions used, however, may well change to accommodate the new dimensions of daily living:

May your lift-offs be smooth and
may you always descend to level terrain.

May enough force always be with you.

May the rings of Saturn
encircle the newlyweds
like bands of titanium.

Every happiness to you and your
brood on the space colony. We
hope to see you again.

Toasting, be it with wine, water, or other liquids, will be performed with squeezable tubes, and the custom of smashing the
glass will pass—at least for travelers in space. Back on Earth
the environmentalists will toast the population with:

Here's mud in your eye!

It is fervently hoped that humankind will lose none of the
pleasure, the camaraderie, the spirit, associated with toasting. It
would be quite a loss.

Let us toast the fools; but for them
the rest of us could not succeed.

—Mark Twain (1835–1910)

BIBLIOGRAPHY

Barnes, Clive, ed. *50 Best Plays of the American Theatre.* New York: Crown Publishers, Inc., 1969.

Bartlett, John, ed. *Familiar Quotations.* Boston: Little, Brown, 1968.

Bespaloff, Alexis. *The Fireside Book of Wine.* New York: Simon & Schuster, 1977.

Clotho, compiler. *Prosit.* San Francisco: Paul Elder and Company, 1904.

Copeland, Lewis; and Copeland, Faye. *10,000 Jokes, Toasts and Stories.* New York: Doubleday & Company, 1965.

Coward, Noel. *Play Parade.* New York: Garden City Publishing Company, 1933.

Doxat, John. *The World of Drinks and Drinking.* New York: Drake Publishers, 1972.

Eden, Anthony. *The Memoirs of Anthony Eden.* Boston: Houghton Mifflin Company, 1965.

Eichler, Lillian. *The Customs of Mankind.* New York: Garden City Publishing Company, 1937.

Fuller, Edmund, ed. *Thesaurus of Anecdotes.* New York: Crown Publishers Inc., 1942.

Gassner, John, ed. *20 Best Plays of the Modern American Theatre.* New York: Crown Publishers Inc., 1939–40.

Heineman, William. *Manners, Customs and Observances.* London: 1894.

Henry, Lewis C. *5000 Quotations for All Occasions.* New York: Garden City Publishing Company, 1945.
    Toasts for All Occasions. New York: Doubleday & Company, 1949.

Huston, Mervyn S. *Toasts to the Bride.* Rutland, Vermont: Charles E. Tuttle Company, 1968.

Kirkwood, K. P. *The Diplomat at Table.* Metuchen, New Jersey: Scarecrow Press, 1974.

Koken, John M. *Here's To It!* Cranbury, New Jersey: A. S. Barnes & Company, 1960.

McClure, John. *The Stag's Hornbook.* New York: Alfred A. Knopf, 1918.

Marchant, W. T. *In Praise of Ale.* London: George Redway, 1888.

Mencken, H. L. *A New Dictionary of Quotations.* New York: Alfred A. Knopf, 1952.

Mew, James; and Ashton, John. *Drinks of the World.* 1892. Reprint. Ann Arbor, Michigan: Gryphon Books, 1971.

Murphy, Edward F., ed. *The Crown Treasury of Relevant Quotations.* New York: Crown Publishers Inc., 1978.

Nehrt, Ardith. *International What's What, When and Where.* Wichita, Kansas: Shawnee Publishing Company.

Newman, Ernest. *Stories of the Great Operas.* New York: Alfred A. Knopf/Garden City Publishing, 1930.

The Oxford Dictionary of Quotations. New York: Oxford University Press, 1953.

Peter, Lawrence J. *Peter's Quotations.* New York: William Morrow & Company, 1977.

Post, Elizabeth L. *The New Emily Post Etiquette.* New York: Funk & Wagnalls, 1975.

119

Prochnow, H. V. *The Speaker's Treasury of Stories for All Occasions*. Englewood, New Jersey: Prentice-Hall, Inc., 1953. *The Toastmaster's Handbook*. Englewood, New Jersey: Prentice-Hall, Inc., 1949.

Rosenberg, M. S. *Quotations for the New Age*. Secaucus, New Jersey: Citadel Press, 1978.

Stevenson, Burton Egbert, ed. *The Home Book of Quotations*. New York: Dodd, Mead & Company, 1967.

Toor, Frances. *Treasury of Mexican Folkways*. New York: Crown Publishers Inc., 1947.

Van Buren, Maud. *Quotations for Special Occasions*. New York: H. W. Wilson, 1939.

Vanderbilt, Amy. *Etiquette*. New York: Doubleday & Company, 1972.

Waugh, Alec; and Time-Life Books. *Foods of the World (Wine and Spirits)*. New York: Time, Inc., 1968.

Wavell, A. P. *Other Men's Flowers*. New York: G. P. Putnam's Sons, 1945.

Wilson, Ellen G. *West African Cook Book*. New York: M. Evans & Company, 1971.

Wood, John R.; and Serres, Jean. *Diplomatic Ceremonial and Protocol*. New York: Columbia University Press, 1970.

DATE DUE			